MW00874232

Tea Thyme
Tea Room

Catherine Delong

Copyright © 2019 Catherine Delong

All rights reserved.

ISBN: 9-78170945-287-1

DEDICATION

This book is in memory of

John Fank

My brother John Fank came to the Bunn House after I had been open for several months and was on my third or fourth cook already. John said he was on vacation from his job of maintenance at a local hotel and said he could help fix the side steps for me.

John came back the next day and started cooking and never left. John was my rock during the very rough first years. John worked with me six days a week while we were in the Bunn House. John never called in sick or asked for time off, taking only one week off a year for vacation.

John moved to Tea Thyme downtown when we closed the Bunn House, and again when we moved to Springfield Clinic. For you that do not know, I am sad to say that John passed away from cancer shortly after Tea Thyme was closed in Springfield Clinic in 2016. I still think of him every day and miss him.

CONTENTS

Introduction

For those that have not heard of Tea Thyme, we opened in 1999 in the Bunn House in Springfield, Illinois.

The Bunn House was the home of a local family that owned Bunn Capitol, Bunn grocery, and the coffee marker Bunn. Tea Thyme was in this location for around nine years.

This book is not a typical cookbook; this is for recipes served in Tea Thyme only. The reason for this book is that a lot of people asked for our recipes, and I would never give them away. People said they would pay, and I told them that someday I would put them into a book.

The recipes in this book all started from ones we found that we worked with and made a lot bigger than the originals. I have tried to cut them back down to ones you can use at home.

I tried to list where the original recipes came from if I knew. With as many years as we were open and through several cooks, I do not know. So I am sorry to anyone that thinks I have their recipe and did not give them credit. If you think so, let me know, and I will include your names and bring this up to date.

This book is not about a Guide on How To. It is not about History or Tradition. It is not about tea from around the world or how to make the best cup of tea. It might not even be the most straightforward cookbook you have ever read though I have tried to make it clear.

This book is more of my memoirs about opening the Tea Thyme Tea Room. I am retired now, and it's been fun thinking about all the good and the bad times. This book is for more sentimental value than for making money thou making some would be nice.

I am giving you a cookbook about recipes served in a real restaurant that were our customer's favorites.

I hope you enjoy reading this book as much as I have enjoyed writing it.

Have fun making your favorite recipe from Tea Thyme at home.

This picture is for an afternoon tea in the private upstairs room. It had one table in that room that would sit up to 12 people. Very popular for a shower.

Tea Thyme Tea Room

The History

I opened the first Tea Thyme Tea Room in 1999. I started working on it in January, going part-time at my day job. I remember our first day open in March; the weather was so lovely. We had flowers on the railings on the front porch and lace with lights. It then snowed, it looked beautiful, but we had to go out and shake the snow off the decorations.

Tea Thyme ended up in three different locations on 6th Street. I must have been insane. Everyone said, come downtown; you will do great. Business was so good in the eight years in the Bunn House. I thought it would be nice to have two locations. The Abraham Lincoln Museum had opened the year before, and I thought we would get a lot of business from that.

The problem was it was very seasonal, and we could not pay the bills in the winter. We only had two parking spaces in front, so customers from the Bunn House location would not come downtown. After several months of running two sites, my husband said I needed to pick one. I did not realize how slow it would be downtown (as our opening was grand). I picked downtown.

One of several significant problems was that with closing the Bunn House, we lost our tour buses because they could not park close to where we were located downtown. Also, the Bunn house had a lot of history. Another big one was people leaving the Museum walked across the street from us as they were going downtown and would already have eaten before coming back to their cars on our side of the street. Also, the

Museum had a café in it, so a lot of people ate there and then left downtown. It turned out very seasonal and was rough those several years. I had changed the name of this location to Tea Thyme Restaurant in hopes of getting more men and families in.

Springfield Clinic offered me a location in their new building. We opened our third location in June of 2013. I again changed the name to Tea Thyme Café. We changed the menu a lot for speed as employees only had a half-hour lunch, and we needed to feed them fast. Also, we had a lot of the same customers every day. We started serving specials and a salad bar with the best-selling sandwiches from our other locations, adding baked goods and breakfast to our menu.

Acknowledgments

I have a lot of people to thank for the many years that Tea Thyme was open. I apologize to anyone I have forgotten.

Special thanks to my husband, Ray, for putting up with me during this time. No dinners for him, long hours of me gone.

Special thanks to my daughter Melinda and her husband, Bryce Bilyeu. Mindy came and worked every Saturday for years, and Bryce came many times to help on holidays when we were short of help. When I was short on servers, Mindy had plenty of college friends that helped, and I want to thank them for dropping everything to help for a day here and there.

Special thanks to my best friend, Kathy Dodd. Kathy was always there when I needed her to help or in prayer. Kathy ended up being my dessert bakery for many years and then opened Tea Thyme Gifts & Things in the small house next to the Bunn house. Unfortunately, she could not find a shop by Tea Thyme when we moved downtown, and she ended up opening a shop on MacArthur for many years. I miss seeing her every day.

Thanks to my sister Teena Knollenberg, she was also a rock in my first years. Teena came in and cleaned the restaurant every day and helped with food on holidays that we were open.

Thanks to my nephew David Fank he is the only person that was with me the whole time we were open. David started working for me in January of 1999 (and Teena also) cleaning all the chairs that I had purchased used from all kinds of small gift shops and barns. We had over 100 chairs, so it was a tremendous job. Also special thanks to my husband Ray, for repairs to chairs regluing and nailing them sturdy. It took weeks for David to hand wash all the new dishes and glasses I purchased and helped clean the Bunn House. David started helping John cook and was a big help.

Special thanks to my friend Pauline Haas she was there to talk to and lean on. Pauline called me all the time to make sure I was ok. I miss seeing her since I have moved away.

Many thanks to the rest of my sisters, brothers, nieces, and nephews. Special thanks to Michelle Marcy for her help. You all came for a few days or months while you were between jobs or on vacation. I thank you all and appreciate the support that you gave. I am sorry that I missed out on all the family events because I was working all the time.

A special thanks to my sister Patty. I gave Tea Thyme to Patty and my brother John when it was at Springfield Clinic. They owned Tea Thyme Cafe and ran it for the last several years it was open.

Thanks to all the employees that I had over the years. There are too many to name, but I still remember a lot of you and hope you have good memories of your time working for me.

But most of all I want to thank all of my customers.

I loved it that you came and spent your lunch breaks with me. I had one customer I teased because she came six times one week. You know who you are. Also, your friend from work (Dentist office) you both came several times a week, every week for years when we were in the Bunn House. I want to thank all the customers that had their bridal showers, baby showers, and even a few weddings with us. I loved planning your parties and making them unique for you.

Sunporch downstairs dining room.

1 CHAPTER BREAKFAST

<u>Secret</u> – In The Bunn House, we only served breakfast for Bridal Showers and Baby Showers. It was nothing for us to have three or four parties in a day beside our regular lunches. Sometimes we had to open on Sunday afternoons to get all the parties done that people wanted to have with us.

Here is a picture of a party's food served as a Buffet in the main dining room.

Ham and Spinach Quiche

6 Servings

1	cup	chopped ham
1 ½	tsp	olive oil
1	small	bag of fresh spinach
½	cup	chopped onion, (1 medium)
2	cups	shredded pepper jack cheese
1	c	milk
2		eggs
1	c	flour
¼	salt	

Heat oven to 400.

Lightly spray 9-inch glass pie pan with cooking spray.

In a skillet heat oil over medium heat, add ham and onions cooking 5 minutes stirring until browned. Spoon mixture into the pan, add spinach on top.

In a bowl, stir milk, eggs, salt, and flour then pour over ham and spinach mixture. Top with the cheese.

Bake 25 to 35 minutes or until knife inserted in center comes out clean. Let stand 10 minutes before cutting.

The quiche was a favorite dish. We served it for breakfast parties at the Bunn House and our downtown location. We then served it for specials at Breakfast and lunch at our Springfield Clinic location.

I also served **Biscuits and Sausage Gravy**. We used a white pepper gravy mix from Farmer Bros Coffee. Then added Bob Even hot sausage to the recipe on the package. Fry the sausage and blend into the gravy using the little bit of grease, It makes the best gravy.

SCRUMPTIOUS EGGS

This recipe makes 12 Servings.

> We built in a restaurant pan, but you could use 2 to 3 pie or cake pans.

2 lbs.	shredded cheese
1½ lbs	fresh mushrooms sliced
1 large	onion chopped
1 stick	butter melted
1 ½	cup cubed ham
17	eggs
2 ½ c	of milk
1/3 c	of flour

Sauté mushrooms and onions in butter until tender; place in pan. Add ham cubes into the pan.

In a bowl, beat eggs with a mixer on high for several minutes, then add milk, then flour.

Pour into pans covering ham and mushroom mixture. Add ½ the cheese.

Bake at 350 for 30 minutes, then top with remaining cheese. Return to oven for 10 minutes. Should be lightly browned, not too dark.

We did a lot of Bridal Shower Brunch. Most parties wanted this dish, and we served it with our French Toast with Banana Rum sauce (see dessert for recipe) and bacon or sausage on the side. Some add a small fruit plate, of course, cake honoring the occasion.

Chapter Two – Lunch – Soups and Salads

Ready for Supper

Main Dining room ready for lunch.

Soups

I do not have exact recipes on our soups. John made them from scratch in the early years and did not write them down. When we got busy, he did not have time for that, so we learned what other restaurants do.

Secret Use a cream base from a restaurant supply store.

On the cream soup, you can go to Gordon Foods store or Sam's Club and buy packages of white cream base. That is your base for any cream soup. You can add cheese and vegetables to make many different soups.

Here is some information on soups.

On the white base (example), the package will tell you two cups of water, for best results mix one cup of cold water in a bowl with a wire whip till smooth. Then pour that mixture into one cup of boiling water on the stove. That is how easy it is to start your soup.

Potato Soup, you would cut up baking potato (stays firm longer) peel or not depending on what you like. Chop up celery, onions, carrots, and boil them with the potatoes till almost done. Do not use the water that the vegetables are cooking in. It is starchy. In the white base, put in some chicken bouillon (we used a soft like butter that was easy to add into the white cream base). Or you can use cubes or liquid.

When your vegetables are finished cooking, you can now add them to your white soup mix and stir. It is that easy. Serve with bacon pieces, shredded cheese, and green onions sprinkled on top.

Cream of Broccoli

You do the same as the Potato soup except you cook broccoli instead of potatoes. On this soup, I would use the broth from cooking the broccoli as the cup of hot water as it will give your soup more flavor. Some people might like some other vegetables in it. You will use the chicken bouillon again.

Remember when cooking any vegetables not to get them to well done. They will still be cooking in your pan of white sauce or while you are holding on a hot stove.

Cream of Celery

Same as Potato soup, only just celery. Using the water, you cooked the celery in for the water for the soup base. Also, the chicken bouillon.

Cream of Mushroom

Same as Potato except you need to slice mushrooms and then boil then for a few minutes. Then throw away that water, do not add to your base; it will not taste as good and made your soup dirty looking (You could use a small amount). So this soup is base, mushroom, and chicken bouillon only. Big mushrooms make a pretty looking soup.

Cream of Asparagus

The same instructions as Cream of Celery.

Tomato and Basil Soup

Yield: 6 servings

1/3 c	olive oil
1	medium onion, chopped
1 t	minced garlic
1/3 c	flour
1	14-ounce can diced tomatoes
2	14 ½-ounce cans chicken broth
2 t	dried basil
½ t	salt
½ t	pepper

Heat olive oil in a large saucepan, sauté onion, and garlic. Stir in flour.

Add remaining ingredients.

Blend well with a wire whisk.

Simmer for 30 minutes, stirring frequently.

Pour into a food processor and puree until smooth.

Pour back into pan until ready to serve.

This soup is even better made ahead and reheated.

John used this recipe from the Junior League of Saint Louis.

Chicken Noodle

We sold a lot of chicken noodle soup. In Illinois, you cannot reheat the soup. So John would cook a pot of noodles and then run cold water over them. Then put in water and store in an airtight container. Then John would cook chicken chunks and vegetables and store them in another airtight container. That way, they were never leftovers. He made several batches of this each week. We served Chicken Noodle every day.

So when you are ready to serve, you mix the two batches together and heat and serve. Always fresh and tasty.

When making chicken noodles, you need an excellent noodle that will not break down. (Or you could make your own.) We used the ones from Sam's Club in a big bag. Sorry, I do not remember the name.

Remember to use a chicken base, noodles, and any vegetables, like celery and carrots.

Lobby going to upstairs dining rooms.

Pumpkin Soup Yield 6 cups

¼ c	butter
1 c	chopped onion
1	clove garlic, crushed
1 t	curry powder
1/8 t	salt
1/8 t	ground coriander
1/8 t	red pepper
3 c	chicken broth
1	16 oz. can pumpkin
1 c	half-and-half
	Sour Cream and chives

In a large saucepan, melt butter: sauté onion and garlic until soft.

Add curry powder, salt, coriander, and red pepper; cook one minute.

Add broth; boil gently, uncovered, for 15 minutes.

Stir in pumpkin and half-and-half; cook 5 minutes.

Pour into blender container. Cover; blend until creamy.

Serve warm or reheat to the desired temperature.

Garnish with sour cream and chopped chives.

John got his recipe out of the St. Louis Days Junior League of St. Louis cookbook.

Secret

The rest of the soups that we served were from Gordon Foods, a store on the west side of Springfield. They sold them in frozen blocks. A few we used were Chili, Beef Stew, and Clam Chowder. You thaw and heat to serve.

Seven Layer Salad

1 head Lettuce chopped
1 small onion chop
   Celery chop
1 frozen bag peas
   bacon bits
1 16 oz. bag shredded cheese
Miracle Whip

This salad is one recipe you assemble by what you like. After chopping ingredients, arrange in even layers. Start with lettuce, sprinkle the onion, celery, peas, and bacon bits on top. Make several layers like that, then top with Miracle Whip, and then cover with cheese.
Cover and keep cold till served.

Our Seven-layer salad was a popular dish at Springfield Clinic as one of the weekly specials and on the salad bar.

Arbor was going into sunporch with summer flowers.

Apple, Dried Cherry, and Walnut Salad
With Maple Dressing

Maple Dressing

2 c	mayonnaise
2 c	pure maple syrup
1/2c	vinegar – white wine or champagne
3 oz	sugar
4 C	vegetable oil

In a bowl, whisk mayonnaise, maple syrup, vinegar, and sugar.

Gradually whisk in oil until mixture thickens slightly.

Keep cold, can use for 2 to 3 weeks.   Makes half gallon

Salad Ingredients

Spring Mix
Dried Cherries, or any fruit you like
Chopped walnuts
Apple slices

Put spring mix on a plate add other ingredients to dress up your dish. Put maple dressing on the side or pour on salad. Serve with a bowl of hot soup and a muffin.

I do not know where we got this recipe but started using it in 2008.

Secret – Use Pure maple syrup. Pancake syrup will not give you as good a flavor.

Chef Salad

That was a favorite salad served with a muffin.
It had a combination of lettuce, Turkey, Ham, tomatoes, black olives, cheese, mushrooms, bacon bits, croutons, and red onion slices.

The Chef salad we served with a Balsamic Vinaigrette that we purchased from MJ Kellner. Sorry do not remember the brand, but Sam's Club used to have one that was close.

Fresh Fruit salad

We started the plate out with a scoop of our Chicken Salad, Tuna Salad, or Seafood Salad on a bed of lettuce. Every day we cut fresh fruit for this. On the side of the plate, we had fresh pineapple, apple slices, strawberries, grapes, melon, and any other fruit we could get from Sam's Club. Then we served that with a side of our cream cheese that we served on the Banana Rum Puffs. People also received a Toffee Rum Muffin.

I have to admit I loved this plate But we were so glad when winter came so we could stop cutting so much fruit.

Spinach Salad

This salad was a big favorite at all three of our locations.

Start with fresh baby spinach, red onion slices, mushroom slices, and Feta cheese. We served with Warm Bacon Dressing. We also put one of our famous Toffee Muffins with it. (See muffins under desserts.)

Secret

When we opened, we tried making the bacon dressing, and I was not happy with it. So shortly after, we started serving one we purchased from the restaurant supply store from Decatur IL. Hoelting Foods. Sorry, I do not remember the name brand of bacon dressing. Shortly before Tea Thyme location closed at Springfield Clinic, the supple store could not get the dressing shipped to Illinois anymore because no other restaurant used it, and we did not buy enough at the Clinic.

So we were using one that you get at a grocery store. It was right above premade salads. Just remember to serve it warm and add your favorite muffin.

The new salads were.

Grilled chicken breast Caesar salad. You all know how to make that.

Also, a **Santa Fe Spinach salad** that had bacon bits, blue cheese, corn, peppers, and red onion with tortilla chips with Ranch dressing and salsa.

Secret

The bread and buns we used we purchased from a bakery and delivered, from Alpha Baking Co. You can buy bread that is a lot like what we used at Sam's Club.

We served **Turkey or Honey Baked Ham** on Rye with Herb Cream Cheese, leaf lettuce, and red onions. Serve this with a fresh salad or fruit.

Italian Beef sandwich

We purchased a large beef from Sam's Club or MJ Kellner, a food company in Springfield. Then John cooked that for hours and cooled. The next day he would tear it into pieces

Secret. Before he cooked the beef, he put on salt and pepper, garlic, and fennel seed. The fennel seed is what gave us the great taste. You have to try this several times to get amounts for your family's needs.

We served it on a fresh bun with au jour and a side salad.

This **beef** is what we served on the dinner menu. John would slice this into big slices instead of tearing it apart. We served it with au jour also.

Chicken Salad with Almonds and Grapes - Here is people's favorite thing on our menu.

John cooked the chicken for the first couple of years we were opened, but it became too much, so he tried a different recipe. No one seemed to notice, so we kept it.

The second recipe John used chicken that was already cooked and cut into cubes. John processed 25-pound boxes of chicken at a time, and he made 2 to 3 batches a week.

You can buy smaller bags of the precooked and cut up chicken at your local grocery in the frozen section.

Thaw the chicken in your refrigerator. Sprinkle chicken with a little garlic salt and curry powder first. Cover and refrigerate overnight for the curry to sink into the meat while it is thawing. (If you cook the chicken, put it on before cooking.)

BIG SECRET.
Everyone asked for this recipe, and we never gave it out. People tried making it, and it did not taste the same. The secret is we used ¾ mayo to ¼ whip cream. The whipped cream is what gave it a different texture. We used Rich's Whip cream that they have in a tube in the freezer section at Gordon Foods.

I cannot give you exact measurements; John never measured it out. After the whipped cream and mayo put in sliced almonds and cut white grapes in ½ and mix it all together and cool before serving. We served this on a croissant with leaf lettuce. Serve with a salad or fresh fruit plate. Have fun trying this one.

Portabella Mushroom

Another favorite. John would clean out the stem and brush mushroom with olive oil and heat on a grill. The Portabella was served with provolone cheese on a croissant with red onion slices.

Secret

After a couple of years, we added on a **Pulled Pork sandwich** served on a bun.

The Pork was a precooked and frozen product from Rich's Foods. We purchased this from Roberts Food, MJ Kellner, or Gordon Foods.

Sam's and Gordon Foods also have some in a tin in the freezer section that is a lot alike.

Tea Thyme served this on a bun with a side salad.

Seafood Sandwich.

Seafood was crab meat and shrimp that we purchased from MJ Kellner. You can buy small packages of both at Walmart frozen section. John added mayo and a few spices, sorry do not know what. But a lot of people liked this sandwich.

We served it on a croissant with leaf lettuce and a side salad.

We moved to Springfield Clinic main campus we added three new sandwiches at that location. We also started serving daily special like hamburgers, lasagna, and other comfort foods.

Bourbon Steak Wrap was a new addition, it was a Philly steak with red peppers grilled, with cheese, lettuce, and tomato served on a garlic herb tortilla.

Also, a **Chicken Chipotle on a Ciabatta bun** served with Chili Chipotle sauce, lettuce, tomato, and red onion.

A popular one was our new **Hot Ham, and Cheese served on a Pretzel Bun.** John would slice several pieces of ham in half and put cheese (maybe pepper jack or swiss) in between. Then grill it, while that was cooking, he would put real melted butter on the bun and heat that also on the grill. Then it would have lettuce and tomato on it and maybe pickles. Serve with soup or salad.

Tea Thyme Café Dining Room at Springfield Clinic

Secret - When we moved downtown, we named the new location Tea Thyme Restaurant. We were hoping to get more men and business people in. We had found out that Tea Room does not bring in a lot of men. We did have a few men that came to Afternoon Tea at the Bunn House with their wives and liked it, and one couple drove from over an hour away.

Entrance to sunporch – Christmas flowers

Apple Chutney

3 c	Red wine vinegar *or* 24 oz.
1 T	Salt
2 ½ c	Brown Sugar
3 T	Mustard Seed

In a pan, bring to a boil the above items.

Add: #10 can apples diced
             2 c   finely chopped onions
             4 c   Raisins
             Grated rind and juice of one lemon

Simmer for two or more hours.

The chutney should simmer until it is of a jam-like consistency. Stir from time to time to prevent scorching.

It can be frozen or poured into sterilized jars, seal as for jam with a thin layer of paraffin, cover, label, and store in a cool place.

We served Apple Chutney over pork at dinners parties. We purchased a huge pork loin and slowly cooked then sliced it like a steak. Add garlic mashed potatoes, vegetables, and fresh biscuits, and you have a great meal.

Tea Thyme started using this recipe in 2005.

Apricot-Glazed Chicken

12 servings

4 T	extra-virgin olive oil
4 lb.	chicken tenderloins, cut in half across on an angle
1	large onion, chopped
4 T	cider or white wine vinegar
25	dried pitted apricots, chopped
4 c	chicken stock
2 c	Apricot preserves
6 T	chopped flat-leaf parsley, for garnish

Heat a large skillet with a lid over medium heat adding the oil.

Add chicken.

Season with salt and pepper. Lightly brown the chicken a few minutes on each side, add onions and cook 5 minutes.

Add vinegar to the pan and let it evaporate.

Add apricots and the stock. When stock comes to a bubble, add preserves and stir to combine. Cover pan, reduce heat and simmer 10-15 minutes.

Serve chicken with a sprinkle of chopped parsley. This pairs nicely with a rice dish and a veggie.

This recipe we started using in December of 2006.

Chicken Basilica

Sorry I cannot find our recipe for this. It was one of my favorites.

I know that we sliced open a boneless piece of chicken. Then we stuffed it with feta cheese. John salt and pepper made a juice of a lemon and other ingredients that I do not remember. The feta cheese cooked inside the chicken with the sauce made this chicken so moist and delicious.

Then bake the chicken till done, around 30 minutes at 350.

After chicken is finished cooking, we would put cold cherry tomatoes, sliced black olives, pine nuts on top, and serve. It was a combo of hot and cold. We served this with wild rice and a vegetable and a hot biscuit.

Big Secret. The **biscuit** we served was close to our scone recipe. That is why they were so good.

Make the biscuit using the scone recipe except do not put the heavy whipping cream and sugar on them halfway thru cooking. When finished baking, brush with melted butter, you could also add a little garlic salt if serving pasta. That is the only difference.

You could mix in some cheese and hot peppers of some kind to come up with another biscuit. Make it your own.

Penne Pasta with Vodka sauce.

1 lb.	Penne Pasta
2 c	Marinara sauce
1	14 ½ oz can diced tomatoes with roasted garlic in juice
1/3 c	chopped fresh basil
¼ c	Vodka
¾ t	dried crushed red pepper
¼ c	freshly grated parmesan cheese

Cook pasta. Meanwhile, heat marinara sauce, tomatoes with juices, basil, and vodka and crushed red pepper until hot.

Add sauce to pasta and toss, transfer to a serving bowl and sprinkle with cheese and serve.

Stuffed Salmon.

The secret, it's so easy. At Roberts Sea Food, we purchased the Salmon. They have an excellent selection. We also purchased from them the stuffing of crab meat. I do not know what all is in it, but everyone loved it.

John put the stuffing on the salmon and baked it. That's all I know for sure. I think he put shredded cheese on top when it was finished cooking. I do not remember, but you can put your favorite on.

Easy dish, thanks to Roberts Sea Food.

Roasted Butternut Squash and Caramelized Onion Tart

Preheat oven to 375

1. Pie Shell – Prick pie shell with a fork all over and sides. Bake shell in the middle of the oven until edge Is pale golden about 20 minutes.

2. Halve 2 -1 lb. Squash (3 ½ pounds. cooked) and scoop out seeds. Lightly brush cut side with oil. Place on a baking sheet cut sides down for 40 minutes, or until soft — the softer, the squash the easier to work with later.

3. Thinly slice one medium onion. In skillet cook in 1 tablespoon butter and 1 tablespoon oil over moderate heat, occasionally stirring until soft and golden brown, about 20 minutes.

4. Cool squash and scoop out the flesh. In food processor puree squash. Add 3 eggs and 1 egg yolk, and 1 cup heavy cream mix well.

5. Stir in
1 c.	Parmesan freshly grated
1 c.	Feta cheese
2 t.	Rosemary
2 t.	Thyme
	Salt & pepper to taste

   Put filling in pie shells

6. In a small skillet, melt 2 T. butter and stir in 1 cup bread crumbs until combined well. Sprinkle crumb mixture evenly over the filling.

7. Place tart in the middle of the oven and bake in a 375 oven for 40 minutes or until filling sets. You should use a pie rim on this to keep crust edge from getting the crust to brown.

Serve Hot. Recipe makes 3 – 9-inch pie pans or 18 servings.

Here are our lobby cash register and tea items for sale.

4 CHAPTER – AFTERNOON TEA

Here is a table ready for Afternoon Tea on the downstairs sun porch.

If you remember, some of the afternoon tea parties and dinners had a man playing the piano during the evening.

That would be Ed Clark Photography and Music Services from Sherman. Ed plays the piano at the Crown Plaza and other events. Ed would play at many parties at the Bunn House and once at Springfield Clinic when we had our Chamber of Commerce ribbon cutting.

DRINKS

Teas we purchased from Coffee Masters.com. They are wholesale only, so I looked at their web page, and they directed me to The Café Connection.com. This online store sells the Ashby's loose and tea bags that we used. They also sell Cocoa Amore hot chocolate that we used. I did not see the Chai tea brand we used but saw David Rio packets of chai that should be pretty good.

They also sell Torani syrup, but the expense on shipping would be high. I purchased Torani at Marquis Beverage.com from Decatur, Illinois. They also carry good coffee and tea products.

I have also purchased Torani at Friar Tuck Beverages on the west side of Springfield, and they have an excellent selection.

I should also mention Farmer Bros Coffee. I miss their coffee; it was delicious. Tea Thyme ordered coffee, and sometimes the tea bags for the three-gallon tea machine from them. I purchased my pepper gravy mix from them; it's great. The best product they have is a #10 can of Hot Fudge. I talked about this in desserts, but theirs is the best in the Springfield area. You can get hot fudge (other brand names) from other food suppliers and Gordon Foods.

Basic Scones

(See next page for ingredients list)

Mix egg and milk in a bowl. Set aside.

Mix dry ingredients, cut in softened butter.

Add the egg/milk mixture, stirring just until moistened. It's not bread; do not knead it will turn out tough. You can overwork this.

Let dough sit for five minutes.

Flour your working table, turn out the dough. Sprinkle dough with a little flour and pat into about 7" circle. Using a 2 ½" biscuit cutter, turn cutter while pushing down. The dough should be about to the top of the cutter. (Do not use a rolling pin.)

Bake in a hot 400-degree oven for 7-8 min.

Then bring scones out of oven and brush tops with heavy cream and lightly sprinkle with sugar. Return to oven for 3-4 minutes. Do not overcook.

Sprinkle with powdered sugar, serve warm.

My original recipe was for 30 scones. I cut this down for your use.

5 Scones

2 c.	Flour
1 T.	Sugar
2 tsp.	Baking Powder
½ tsp.	Baking Soda
3/4 tsp.	Salt
1/4 c.	Butter
1	Egg
2/3 c.	Half & Half

15 Scones

6 c.	Flour
3 T.	Sugar
2 T.	Baking Powder
1 ½ tsp.	Baking Soda
2 ¼ tsp.	Salt
¾ c.	Butter (1 ½ stick)
3	Eggs
2 c.	Half & Half

Devonshire Cream

Chill mixing bowl and beaters first.

Full Batch (5 cups)

1 c	cold water
2 t.	Unflavored gelatin
2 c	Heavy Whipping Cream
4 t.	Vanilla
½ c.	Sugar
2 c	Sour Cream

Mix gelatin in cold water. Set aside for 10 minutes. Then heat (10 seconds) in the microwave until gelatin is clear. Do not overheat. Stir and set aside.

Add heavy cream in a chilled bowl. Beat on high speed until stiff add vanilla and sugar and continue beating until stiff.

In a small bowl, add sour cream and gelatin water. Stir until well blended and smooth, then stir in whipped cream. DO NOT BEAT.

Chill 1 hour before serving. Store in an airtight container. Never stir. It will break it down. It is usual for some water to form at the bottom of the bowl after several days. Leave it alone. Scoop it out from top to serve.

Discard unused Devonshire after one week.

Lemon Curd

Full Batch size

2c	butter (1 lb. / 4 sticks)
8	eggs
2 c	Lemon Juice
3 c	Sugar

(Makes about 2 quarts)

Melt butter in a double boiler.

While butter is melting, mix eggs, lemon juice, and sugar in a separate bowl. Slowly add the mixture to butter before it's all melted. Mix well and stir.

Cook mixture approximately 20 minutes will be the consistency of a thin pudding. Turn off heat and let sit; it will finish cooking with the hot water under it. If you have egg (cooked) pieces, stain them out while still warm. Let cool and refrigerate in an airtight container.

Discard remaining curd after two weeks.

Small Batch
1 c butter (2sticks)
4 eggs
1 c Lemon juice
1 ½ c Sugar

Of course, you serve this with Scones. But this is also good for cake and other desserts. I do not remember where I got this recipe in 1999.

We also served **finger sandwiches and finger desserts at Afternoon Tea.** Those are many we just made up or were mini of items we already made.

Some of the sandwiches were mini of Chicken Salad on a small Puff Pastry. Cucumber sandwiches also rolled up sandwiches on flatbreads with cream cheese and meats and cheeses.

Some of the desserts were mini Lemon bars, small "American Scones," brownie bites, cakes, and mini pie and cookies. Of course, it came with freshly baked scones with the Lemon Curd and Devonshire Cream.

5 CHAPTER - DESSERT

Kathy Dodd baked our desserts till she opened her own Tea Thyme Gift & Things shop in the little house in the side yard of the Bunn House.

Here is a picture of a cake that Kathy made for a party held at Tea Thyme Tea Room.

If you know Kathy, you know that she makes the best Apple Raisin Pie in the world.

Apple Crisp

We used a #10 can of apples because we sold a lot of this dessert. But you could peel and cut up fresh apples.

You can half or quarter this recipe to make it smaller. You really cannot get this wrong. Add pecans, raisins, or change cinnamon and nutmeg to your tastes.

Topping

Combine in bowl

10 T	cold butter, cut into pieces
1 c	packed brown sugar
1 c	flour
1 c	oatmeal
1 T	cinnamon
1 T	nutmeg

Work together with fingers until the mixture resembles a coarse meal.

Put apples into the pan, add pecans or raisins if you want, then spoon topping over top of apples.

Bake till top is brown around 30 to 45 minutes. Test apples to see if they are tender.

Serve hot with ice cream or whip topping.

For a twist, if you make the Rum Sauce recipe use it instead of whip topping. Yum

Apricot and Cherry Crisp

Preheat oven to 400

 Grease an 8x8 inch baking dish with butter.

For the Filling: In a large bowl, mix the ingredients, then pour into pan.

2 ½ pounds	apricots, peeled, pitted sliced half-inch thick
1 pound	cherries pitted
¾ cup	sugar
¼ cup	flour
2 T	butter

In a separate bowl, mix the topping ingredients.

1 cup	oatmeal
¾ cup	flour
¾ cup	brown sugar
½ cup	butter, melted
1 t	cinnamon
1 t	salt

Pour onto the fruit mixture and bake for 25 minutes, or until the topping is golden brown. Remove from the oven and cool for 15 minutes before serving.

Recipe yields eight servings.

Note my husband decided one year to grow cherries for our use. Poor Kathy pitted them one day with a machine he had for her to use. Kathy had cherry juice all over the kitchen and herself. But we had the best fresh cherry pie ever that year.

Banana Cake

2 c	flour
½ t	baking powder
¾ t	baking soda
½ t	salt
1 ½ c	sugar
½ c	butter, melted
2	eggs
1 t	vanilla
¼ c	buttermilk or yogurt
1 c	mashed ripe bananas
½ c	chopped walnuts (opt.)

In one bowl, mix all dry ingredients, then set it aside. In a large mixing bowl, add all wet ingredients, beating on low until well blended.

Gradually add dry mixture to wet mixture, beating on low speed and scraping sides of the bowl.

Mix on medium speed for two minutes

Put into prepared cake pans and bake 350 until a wooden toothpick inserted in the middle comes out clean.

One batch makes 9 x13 cake pan or 24 cupcakes
Cake = approx. 30 + minutes to bake.
Cupcakes = approx. 15 – 20 minutes.

Hint: something different in making these Banana cupcakes, put half the batter into the cupcake paper. Then add half teaspoon of Raspberry jam, then add more mixture on top of the jam. Bake and cool a few minutes before eating. That jam is hot.

(Kathy Dodd's recipe from March 2005)

Banana Rum Sauce- Double Batch

Biggest Secret
A lot of people tried to make this and could not. That is because you have to have the correct Rum. We used Captain Morgan spiced rum. Other rum will not give you the same flavor.

8 sticks of butter
4 # of brown sugar (not packed) or (2 bags 2 lbs.)
10 egg yolk
3 C of water
1 C Captain Morgan spiced rum

In a large double boiler pan, melt the butter slowly over low heat.

In a bowl separate egg yolks, Stir water into a bowl, add brown sugar mix well. (Reserving whites for later use in a different recipe, can be frozen)

Add yolk mixture into melted butter. Cook and continuously stir over medium-low heat for 5 to 10 minutes till mixture boils.
The sauce can burn very quickly and will then have brown specks in it. You can still use it if it's not bad.
Remove from heat and stir in rum. Cool, stirring several times to keep butter well mixed together. Serve warm or cool it stirring several times and then refrigerated till use.

Note: I started using the Banana Rum Sauce in Sept of 1999. The first time we made it was for a Bridal Shower. Someone wanted breakfast, and I did not want to serve just French Toast with maple syrup, so this is a recipe we found somewhere and worked on it, and it became the most popular item on our menu. We sold it by the cup to favorite customers.

We used this on French Toast with Bananas slices, on the Banana Rum Puff dessert, and also Bread Pudding with Rum Sauce.

To make our Banana Rum Puff, you need to make the Rum Sauce and the Cream Cheese filling recipe listed in this book first.

Then you need to bake the puff pastry.

Here is a picture of Banana Rum and Cherry Puff. These are smaller sizes served on a buffet table.

About Puff Pastry

<u>Secret</u>
We purchased the puff pastry sheets from the restaurant food service. It is a Pillsbury product. It comes in a large sheet, and you cut the sheet into the size you want then bake them. After you cook the puff pastry sliced each piece into three pieces to build the puff.

On the bottom layer, you spread the cream cheese. Put the middle piece of puff on top of that. Then you slice about ½ a banana on top of the middle section. Then pour some warm Rum sauce on top of the bananas. Then put the lid back on and sprinkle powdered sugar.

I found a puff pastry sheet in the grocery store frozen sections you can buy. It is Pepperidge Farm, and I tried it, and it is good. Puff was folded in thirds, and you can thaw and open after about 20 minutes. Then cut on the fold line, then cut the three pieces into the size you want. Tea Thyme size was half so that a sheet would give you six parts, but cutting into three each would also be a good size. Then finish thawing, about 40 minutes total. Sheets should still be cold.
Or you can make the puff pastry yourself. I do not include a recipe since we did not make the pastry.

Cherry Puff

We needed a dessert for people that did not like bananas. So we came up with the Cherry Puff. So instead of the bananas and rum sauce, just put canned cherry pie filling on the second layer instead.

Banana Split Puff

Or change it up, put the bananas crushed pineapple, and fresh sliced strawberries. We did not use the rum sauce; we just put extras cream cheese on the bottom layer.

Cream Cheese filling

Used on Tea Thyme Puff Pastries

This recipe is 1/3 of the original recipe. You can also use this as cake icing by adding more powdered sugar to make it thicker. It is excellent on Banana or Carrot cake too.

2 lb.	Cream cheese at room temperature.
2 sticks	butter at room temperature.
1 1/2 T	vanilla
2 lb.	powdered sugar

With an electric mixer, cream the butter.

Gradually add cream cheese mixing well after each addition until well blended, so no cheese chunks remain, should be smooth.

Add vanilla

Slowly add powdered sugar. Mix until creamy. Store in airtight containers in the refrigerator until ready to use. Serve cold.

Bread Pudding

<u>*One - ½* pan *serves* 12 *people*</u>
13	eggs
5 C	milk
1 C	sugar
1 T	cinnamon
1 T	nutmeg
1 T	vanilla

bread cubes approx. 10+ cups
    1 C raisins (on top only)

Place dry bread cubes in prepared pan, filling to the top of the pan. Set aside.

In bowl, beat eggs. Add sugar, milk, cinnamon, nutmeg and vanilla.

Pour egg mixture evenly over dry bread cubes. Stir then let stand for 10 minutes. Press down gently, so all bread cubes are wet. *Add raisins (Don't mix raisins in as some people do not like them and can take them off)*

Bake 325* approx. 50 min to an hour. Bake until a knife inserted near the center comes out clean. Cool slightly, serve warm (with Rum Sauce). Keep leftovers refrigerated.

See how to make bread crumbs on the next page.

To dry bread cubes, cut up white bread or buns into cubes and bake in a 350* oven for about 15 minutes. Stir and repeat until cubes are dry about 45 minutes.

As Tea Thyme was busier, we could not keep up with drying bread crumbs. We started buying them from Shop & Save in a large bag that made a full sheet pan. We made a full-size pan of bread pudding every day.

We cannot forget one of the most popular desserts, but easy to make.

Brownie Hot Fudge.

We made brownies, box mix from MJ Keller. Then we purchased ice cream squares individual wrapped from Prairie Farms Dairy on 9th St.

The hot fudge we purchased in a #10 can from Farmers Brothers coffee on the west side of Springfield. They have the best flavor.

So put the brownie on the plate, then ice cream, heat the fudge pour over ice cream. Add whip cream and chopped nuts and cherry.

Chocolate Cream Pie

Crust – You need two pie shells cooled.

Filling
Put in a saucepan on a stove on low heat stirring, so it does not stick.

2 c	Sugar
4 c	Milk
½ t	Salt

Mix in a bowl and set aside till cornstarch is smooth.

1 c	Milk
½ c	Cornstarch
8	Egg yolks

4 ounces Chocolate Unsweetened (we used one that was a melted in a package, it's a lot easier)

Get ready and set aside

4 T	Butter
2 t	Vanilla

Once everything is ready, turn up the heat on the saucepan. Watch and stir till the mixture gets hot, then temper the hot mixture into the bowl mixture, then back into the pan and boil for 2 minutes. Take off heat and add the butter and vanilla you set aside.

Divide mixture between 2 pie crusts. Put cling wrap on top of pie and chill for 3 to 4 hours or overnight, so it sets up.

We started using this in Aug of 2008, an unknown original recipe. Chocolate and the Coconut Cream pie are the same base. You could use this to make other pie flavors.

Coconut Cream Pie

Crust
1 Pastry Shell – Bake at 400 for 9 to 10 minutes

Filling
¾ c	Sugar
2 ¾ c	Milk

Put milk and sugar in a saucepan on the stove on low heat. Stirring, so it does not stick.

Mix in a cup stirring until cornstarch is smooth, then set this aside.
¼ c	Milk
4	Egg Yolks
¼ c	Cornstarch

Get this ready and set aside
1 c	Coconut
1 t	Vanilla
1 T	Butter

When the above is already turn up the heat and watch and stir saucepan on the stove. Bring the milk to the boiling point and temper some into the egg yolk cup. Then pour back into the pan of hot milk. Whisk until smooth, and the mixture is thick, stirring constantly.

Remove the pan from the heat and stir in coconut, butter, and vanilla.

Pour into pie shell and cover with film and cool about 10 minutes then put in the refrigerator.

Cream Puffs

Preheat oven to 400
1 c	Water
½ c	Butter (1 stick)
1 c	Flour
	Pinch nutmeg
4	eggs

In saucepan heat water and butter to a rolling boil
Stir in 1 cup flour and pinch nutmeg

Stir vigorously over low heat until mixture forms a ball, about one minute.

Remove from heat. Then beat in 4 eggs continue beating till smooth

Drop dough by ¼ cup about 3 inches apart onto an ungreased cookie sheet.

Bake at 400 for 35-40 minutes until puffed and golden

Cool away from a draft.

When cool, you can cut them in half and pull out any soft dough inside.

Now you can add a yummy cream in the middle (see next page for a recipe), then put the top back on and put powdered sugar on it.

You can also use the lemon curd recipe inside puffs. But lemon curd should be warmed first.

Cream Filling for Puffs

1/3 c	sugar
2 T	cornstarch
1/8 t	salt
2 c	milk
2	egg yolks, slightly beaten
2 T	butter softened
2 t	vanilla

In a 2-quart saucepan, mix sugar, cornstarch, and salt over medium heat. Stir in milk gradually, stirring until mixture thickens and boils. Boil and stir 1 minute.

Stir at least half of the hot mixture slowly into egg yolks, Blend that back into the hot mixture. Boil and stir 1 minute. Remove from heat; stir in margarine and vanilla.

Cool and then put into cream puffs.

Gooey Butter Cake - Chocolate

Prep time 20 minutes and serves 12 people
Ingredients
1 pkg.   chocolate cake mix
2 sticks   butter
3   eggs
1   8 oz.   pkg. cream cheese
4T   cocoa powder
1 t   vanilla
1 16 oz.   bag of powdered sugar
1 c   chopped nuts

Preheat oven to 350 degrees. Lightly grease 13x9 baking pan.

In mixing bowl, combine the cake mix, one egg, and one stick of melted butter, stir until well blended. Pat mixture into a pan and set aside.

In a mixer, beat the cream cheese until smooth, then add two eggs and cocoa powder. Lower the speed of the mixer and add the powdered sugar. Continue beating until ingredients are well mixed. Slowly add the remaining stick of melted butter and the vanilla, continue to beat mixture until smooth. Stir in nuts with a rubber spatula. Spread filling over cake mixture in pan.

Bake for 50 minutes. The center should still be a little gooey when finished baking. Let cake partially cool before cutting into pieces.

Original recipe from Food Network, we started using April of 2010.

Gooey Butter Cake - Pumpkin

Cake
2	Yellow Cake Mix
2	eggs
16 T	butter, melted

Filling
2	(8 oz.) cream cheese softened
2	cans (15 oz.) pumpkin
6	eggs
2 t	vanilla
16 T	butter, melted
2 lbs.	powdered sugar
2 t	cinnamon
2 t	nutmeg

Directions

Combine cake mix, egg, and butter mix well with mixer. Pat mixture into a large square cake pan (15x11) and set aside.

Beat the cream cheese and pumpkin until smooth. Add eggs, melted butter, and vanilla beat together. Next, add powdered sugar, cinnamon, nutmeg, and mix well.

Spread pumpkin mixture over cake batter and bake for 50 minutes at 350. Make sure not to over bake as the center should be a little gooey.

You can cut this in half for smaller. Also, take out the pumpkin and add a 20 ounce can of pineapple for a different flavor. Tea Thyme used the first time in the fall of 2010.

Holiday Carrot Cake

(Yields, 16 servings)

Preheat oven to 350

Prepare two 9" round pans, sprayed with "Pam."

Combine, beat until light.

2 cups sugar and 1 ½ cup oil

Add 4 eggs one at a time beating well after each addition.

Add

3 c	flour
½ tsp	baking powder
¾ tsp	baking soda
½ tsp	salt
1 T	cinnamon
1 tsp	nutmeg

Beat until smooth.

Stir into the above mixture

2 ½ c	shredded raw carrots
½ c	chopped maraschino cherries
1 ½ c	chopped walnuts
½ c	flaked coconut

Pour into the pans you prepared. Cook for 40 to 50 minutes till done.

Cool in pan for 10 minutes. Invert onto a wire rack to cool completely.

Serve plain or frost with cream cheese frosting.

Key Lime Pie

1 1/2 c	graham cracker crumbs
1/2 c	granulated sugar
4 T	(1/2 stick butter) melted
2	(14 oz) cans condensed milk
1 c	key lime or regular lime juice
2	eggs
1 c	sour cream
2 T	powdered sugar
1 T	lime zest

Preheat your oven to 375 degrees F.

In a bowl, mix the graham cracker crumbs, sugar, and butter with your hands. Press the mixture firmly into a 9-inch pie pan, and bake until brown, about 20 minutes.

Remove from the oven and allow to cool to room temperature before filling. After baking the pie crust, lower the oven temperature to 325 degrees.

In a separate bowl, combine the condensed milk, lime juice, and eggs. Whisk until well blended and place the filling in the cooled pie shell.

Bake in the oven for 15 minutes and allow to chill in the refrigerator for at least 2 hours.

Once chilled, combine the sour cream and powdered sugar and spread over the top of the pie using a spatula. Sprinkle the lime zest as a garnish on top of the sour cream and serve chilled.

Yield: 8 servings

Million Dollar Pie

Crust

2	Pastry Shell - cooled
1	egg yolk

Filling

1	14 oz. can sweeten condensed milk
1/3 c	lemon juice
2	20 oz. cans crushed pineapple - drained
20 oz.	whip topping
1 c	course walnuts
10 oz.	Cherries drained and halved

Crust: Coat crust with beaten egg yolk Bake 3250   Cool 5 minutes.

Filling
Combine milk, lemon juice mix well.
Stir in pineapple, whip topping, walnuts, and all but 16 cherry halves.

Divide mixture between 2 pie crusts decorate with the 16 cherry halves
Let set up overnight for the best results.

This recipe was from a closed tea room that was out on Jefferson St. One of the owners came and cooked for me for a short time and added this to our menu. August 16, 2008 Thanks, Kevin.

Muffins

We baked our own at first, then discovered this fantastic product from Pillsbury.

They make muffins batter in a tube that comes in frozen from the food vendors. Our signature muffin was Butter Rum. It was wonderful. We served that muffin on all the salads, and when we had breakfast parties, come on the plate with eggs or whatever the hostess had ordered.

When we closed the other two locations and moved to Springfield Clinic, we had a Bakery case and served this muffin along with Banana and Blueberry muffins. They were all from the frozen tubes. We just thawed and cooked them.

After I left Tea Thyme, I still baked muffins and other items for meetings for Springfield Clinic, but I used ones that you buy in the store, in a box. I do not think they could tell the difference. The thing that I believe made them good was that before I cooked the muffins, I sprinkled decorating sugar on top. So when they bake the sugar kind of crunches up on the top.

Pineapple Upside-Down Cake

Make a white cake (or your favorite flavor) per package instructions then set aside.

Topping

½ stick	unsalted butter, melted
2/3 c	firmly packed light brown sugar
1 can	Pineapple rings
1 jar	of Cherries

In a small bowl, stir together well the butter and the brown sugar and spread mix evenly in buttered pan. Place pineapple in pan on top of the topping mixture. Put a cherry in the hole of the pineapple ring.

Now pour cake batter into the pan all over the topping and pineapple. Bake in the middle of the oven for 45 to 50 minutes or until a tester comes out clean. Let cake cool in the pan for 15 minutes. Then invert the cake onto your cake plate. Warning, the topping can run down the cake, so watch fingers; it will still be hot.

Red Velvet Cake

Preheat oven to 350. Lightly oil cake pans.

Makes ½ sheet or four 9" cake

Dry Ingredients

5 c	all-purpose flour
3 ½ c	sugar
2 t	baking soda
2 t	salt
2T	cocoa powder

Wet Ingredients

2	large eggs at room temperature
2 c	buttermilk at room temperature
3 c	vegetable oil
4 T	red food coloring (2 ounces)
2 t	white distilled vinegar
2 t	vanilla extract

In a large bowl, sift together the dry ingredients.

In another mixing bowl, whisk together the wet ingredients, blend the dry into the wet ingredients until batter is smooth.

Divide cake the batter evenly among the cake pans, placing pans in the oven, rotating the pans halfway through cooking. Cook about 30 minutes till cake pulls away from the side of the pan. A toothpick inserted in the center of the cakes comes out clean.

Remove cakes from oven and run a knife around the edges to loosen them from the sides of the pans.

(Red Velvet Cake) One at a time, invert the cakes onto a plate. And then re-invert them onto a cooling rack, rounded-side up. Let cool completely.

Place one layer, rounded-side down, in the middle of a rotating cake stand. Using an offset spatula spread some of the cream cheese frostings over the top of the cake. (Spread enough frosting to make a ¼ to ½ inch layer.) Carefully set another layer on top, repeating icing, add the remaining layer, and cover the entire cake with the frosting. Sprinkle top with pecans.

See the next page for Cream Cheese frosting.

Cream Cheese frosting

1 lb.	cream cheese softened
4 c	powdered sugar
2 sticks	butter (1 cup) softened
1 t	vanilla

In a mixer with a paddle attachment, mix the cream cheese, sugar, and butter on low speed until incorporated. Increase the speed to high and mix until light and fluffy, about 5 minutes.

Reduce the speed to low and add the vanilla, then raise the speed too high, and mix briefly until fluffy. Store in the refrigerator until somewhat stiff before using it.

Store in the refrigerator for 3 to 7 days.

Unknown where we found this. Start using in July 2008.

Strawberry Pie

Strawberry Pie is so easy anyone can make it pretty much instant, or you can make your pie shell and glaze from scratch.

Start with a cooked pie shell.

Clean strawberries and cut off green tops. If berries are huge slice in half, you will want some small strawberries whole to make your pie pop.

Then you could make the glaze yourself, but since we did not, I do not include a recipe. We purchased the glaze in a #10 can from food suppliers. But you can go and get a small tub of it by fresh strawberries at your local store.

Smear the strawberry glaze on your cooked pie shell. Then start placing strawberries in pie shell filling it up. Use big ones mostly, then fill in with the smaller ones. Then when you are happy with that smear, a lot of glaze over your whole pie. Cool before serving.

The hardest part of this whole recipe is cutting the pie and placing it on the plate. It does work less messy if you have a strawberry pie cutter from a food supply store, you could try the Gordon Food Store.

Then add whip cream and serve and see happy faces.

Sticky Buns

We used frozen cinnamon rolls. You can buy at your local store like the ones we used, or make your own. The frozen rolls work better than canned. You do need to thaw the cinnamon rolls before baking.

Preheat oven to 350 bake 18 to 30 minutes depending on the size of rolls. You need to use time from the cinnamon roll package as your guideline.

Glaze for 8 Sticky Buns

¾ c	brown sugar
¼ c	honey
¼ c	corn syrup
½ c	water
1	stick of butter
1 c	pecan halves

Beat brown sugar, butter, honey, corn syrup, and water. Pour glaze into a pan, sprinkle pecans on top.

Then place thawed cinnamon rolls on top of the glaze. Bake Sticky Buns until deep golden brown.

Immediately turn hot buns over so sticky, and pecan is on top and place on a platter. Stir glaze left on the bottom of pan and spoon over the rolls. If the glaze is too thick, add a few drops of hot water and stir till texture you want.

Best served warm.

Sugar Cookies small batch

Cream together

1c	butter
1 c	shortening
2 c	sugar

1 t	vanilla add to the above mixture.
4	eggs add to the mix one at a time.

Mix in another bowl

6 c	flour
2 t	baking powder
½ t	salt

Beat the flour mixture into the butter mixture for 3 minutes

Chill dough several hours in the refrigerator before using it.

Preheat oven 350

Then roll out, cut and bake on parchment paper for 10 minutes,   Rotate in the oven, and cook 4-5 more minutes.

Makes 4 dozen cookies

Sugar Cookies Icing

2/3   c water
2 #   bag powdered sugar
1 t.   clear
4 t.   corn syrup

Mix in one bowl with hand beater, pour into additional small containers to add coloring. On a snowman, it would be white icing. A Christmas tree would be green icing.

If you do not wish to frost/ice your cookies, you can put sprinkles on cookies before baking.

Put the 1st coat of icing on after cookies cool. The first coat of frosting needs to dry AT Least 2 HOURS before adding different color icing on top of the first coat. Otherwise, the colors will bleed.

Decorate after the first layer sets up. Colors start running after a day and do not look as beautiful. We always tried to bake as needed.

Sugar Cookies large batch – use the same instructions as a small batch.

Preheat oven 350

Cream together
4c   butter
4c   shortening
8c   sugar
4 t   vanilla   add to above
16 eggs   add to the above mixture one at a time.

Mix in a bowl
24 c   flour
8 t   baking powder
2 t   salt

Makes 16 – 17 dozen cookies depends on what size cookie cutters you use.

Have fun with the large batch; it's big.

The secret on the cookies.

Our baker Neely was trying to make cookies for order; this was about the fourth year we were open. She called her brother, who worked in a restaurant and asked for his help, and he gave her some tips.

Neely tweaked it some and after she left working for Tea Thyme Kathy Dodd, and I tweaked it some more to come up with this exact recipe.

We started getting more and more orders for these. I made them for the last time the first year we were at Springfield Clinic. By this time at Christmas, I was making over 100 dozen batches of cookies, which is over 1,000 cookies. I could not make them fast enough in the one oven we had at that location. I was there at 4 am to put on the final decorations for cookies going out that day. Then when we closed, I started baking again till 10 pm and getting the first coat of icing on the cookies. After several weeks of that, I did not take orders the next year and only made for the clinic's use.

Texas Cake

Preheat oven to 350 (This make two small sheet pans)
Step 1 Combine in a bowl

4 c	flour
4 c	sugar
2 t	baking soda
1 t	salt
½ t	cinnamon
½ c	cocoa

Step 2
In new bowl Combine with a spoon till smooth   (do not use a mixer on this recipe)

1 c	sour cream or buttermilk
4	eggs
2 t	vanilla

Step 3 in a small pan stir after each item.

1	c melted butter (2 sticks)
1 C	oil
2 c	water

Bring Step 3 to boil, take off stove, stir in ingredients from Step 2, then from step 1

Pour batter into two pans 13x9x2 (line with the paper if taking out of the pan) or 3 ½ sheet pan with sides.

Bake 400 for 20 to 25 minutes or until a toothpick is clean.

To cheat, you could use a box cake mix and add cinnamon.

See the next page for icing.

Icing for Texas Cake

While the cake is baking, prepare the frosting, which is the best part.

1 c	milk
½ c	cocoa (8 T)
1 c	Butter
2 lbs.	Powdered Sugar (8 cups)
2 t	Vanilla
2 c	Pecans chopped

Mix the milk and cocoa in a heavy saucepan (stir, stir)
Add the butter and over medium heat stir until the butter melts.

Remove from heat and gradually stir in the sugar and vanilla until smooth. Add Pecans

When the cake is just out of the oven, spread the frosting evenly on the hot cake. It's easiest to pour it around. The icing cools very fast, and if you do not put it on the cake while it is hot, it will start tearing your cake. Work fast to get it frosted.

I do not remember where we started this recipe from; I think we saw it in a newspaper.

Funny story. We did a lot of tour buses. We served this cake to a lot of them, and one bus happened to be from Texas. Customers on the bus said they had never heard of Texas Cake. I live in Texas now, and a lot of people here have never had it.

Here is a picture of Mindy and Bryce Bilyeu working the booth at the Taste of Down Town in 2002.

We did the Springfield Taste of Down Town for around five years. It was always an enjoyable event. We usually served Ice Tea with flavors, chicken salad sandwiches, and our Banana Rum Puff or Cherry Puff.

ABOUT THE AUTHOR

I worked at The Salvation Army Adult Rehabilitation Center on 11th St Springfield, IL, from 1981 to 1999 as Bookkeeper then Administrative Asst.

I wanted to do something different, so I opened the Tea Thyme Tea Room in 1999 until June of 2013. I returned to The Salvation Army Citadel from December 2013 to 2017.

Retired in July 2017 and moved to Lindale, Texas, with husband, Raymond Delong. We have one daughter Melinda who is married to Bryce Bilyeu with the three most exceptional children in the world.

For more pictures or help with a recipe, contact me, Tea Thyme Tea Room facebook page.